AF265592

SUPPLEMENT

TO

BRETT'S

BANKRUPTCY ACT, 1883

CONTAINING

A TABLE SHOWING THE PARTS·OF THE ACT AND RULES WHICH ARE TO BE READ TOGETHER; A SUMMARY OF

THE

Points of importance contained in the Rules,

AND THE

TABLE OF FEES

OF THE 28th DECEMBER, 1883.

LONDON:

BUTTERWORTHS, 7, FLEET STREET,

Law Publishers to the Queen's most excellent Majesty.

DUBLIN: HODGES, FIGGIS & CO., GRAFTON STREET.
CALCUTTA: THACKER, SPINK & CO. MELBOURNE: GEORGE ROBERTSON.
MANCHESTER: MEREDITH, RAY & LITTLER.
EDINBURGH: T. & T. CLARK; BELL & BRADFUTE.

1884

Price 1s. 6d.

LONDON:
PRINTED BY C. F. ROWORTH, BREAM'S BUILDINGS,
CHANCERY LANE—E.C.

TABLE

OF THE

Corresponding portions of the Act and Rules.

———◆———

THE following Table shows the various portions of the
Act and Rules which are to be read together :—

BANKRUPTCY ACT, 1883.	BANKRUPTCY RULES, 1883.
SECT.	RULE
1. Short title of Act	1. Short title of Rules.
3. Commencement of Act	1. Commencement of Rules.
4. Acts of bankruptcy	117. Declaration of inability to pay, with Form No. 3 in Appendix.
	118—124. Bankruptcy notice.
	151. Receiving order on bankruptcy notice.
	191. Proceedings by company or co-partnership.
5. Receiving order	150—154. Receiving order generally.
	195. Receiving order against a firm.
6. Creditor's petition	125—128. Form of petition, &c.
	129—143. Proceedings thereunder.
	144—149. Service, and see rr. 79—83.
	154. Costs of petition, and see rr. 98—110.
	191. Proceedings by company or co-partnership.
	200—202. Proceedings under sect. 125.
7. Proceedings on creditor's petition.	79—83, 144—148. Service.
	39—50. Affidavits.
	129—143. Proceedings.
	30. Security by debtor.
	192—197. Proceedings by or against a firm.
	149. Hearing of petition.
	98—110. Costs.
8. Debtor's petition	The last three groups, read with sects. 5, 6 and 7, are applicable also to debtors' petitions.
9. Effect of receiving order	152. May include stay of proceedings.
10. Discretionary powers of Court thereupon.	152. Stay of proceedings.
	134. Appointment of interim receiver.
11. Service of order staying proceedings.	79—83. Service.

BANKRUPTCY ACT, 1883.	BANKRUPTCY RULES, 1883.
SECT.	RULE
12. Power to appoint special manager.	244. Removal of special manager. 253. Security given by manager. 254. Remuneration.
13. Advertisement of receiving order.	150 et seq. Receiving order. 203. Board of Trade and Gazette. 15. Registrar filing copy.
15. First and other meetings of creditors.	184—190. Meetings of creditors. 199 (7). In small bankruptcies. 13. As to meeting summoned by Court. 207. Record book. 223. Notice of resignation by trustee. 227. Meeting to consider conduct of trustee.
16. Debtor's statement of affairs	168. Statement of affairs, how made out. 237. Official receiver's duties. 238. Special report, when person employed to assist debtor. 196. In case of a partnership.
17. Public examination	5. To be heard in open Court.
18. Composition or scheme of arrangement.	5. Application for approval to be heard in open Court. 159—167. Rules as to composition or scheme of arrangement. 184—190. Meeting of creditors. 199. Small bankruptcies. 183. Proxies and voting letters. 166. Amendment. 203, 204. Gazetting, &c.
20. Adjudication	155—158. Rules as to adjudication. 203, 204. Duty of Board of Trade. 15. Filing, Gazetting, &c. 247. Transfer of property. 248. Accounting by official receiver. 197. Adjudication against partners.
21. Appointment of trustee	218—231. Rules as to. 207—217. Accounts and audit. 251, 252. Payments into and out of bank. 253. Security by trustee. 247. Transfer of property.
22. Committee of inspection	209, 210. Audit of trustee's books and accounts. 228. Application for authority on account at local bank. 250. Rule where no committee of inspection.

BANKRUPTCY ACT, 1883.	BANKRUPTCY RULES, 1883.
SECT.	RULE
23. Power to accept composition or scheme after adjudication.	159—167. Rules as to composition or scheme. 158. As to annulling adjudication. 203, 204. Gazetting, &c. 15. Filing.
24. Duties of debtor as to discovery and realization of property.	77, 78. Applications to commit.
25. Arrest of debtor	75 et seq. Warrants; arrests, &c.; custody of debtor.
27. Discovery of debtor's property.	70. Application for discovery. 64. Discovery. 53—63. Witnesses and depositions.
28. Discharge	5. To be heard in Court. 19—29. Motions and Practice. 178—182. Discharge. 203, 204. Gazetting, &c. 15. Filing.
32. Disqualification of bankrupts	5. To be heard in Court. 19—29. Motions and practice.
35. Power to annul adjudication	158. Order annulling. 203, 204. Gazetting. 15. Filing.
37. Proof of debts	169—174. Proof of debts. 39—50. Affidavits. 84—87. Trial by jury. 5. Applications to be made in Court when over 200*l.*
46. Duties of sheriff as to goods taken in execution.	11. As to notice in writing.
47. Avoidance of voluntary settlements.	5. Application to be heard in Court.
48. Avoidance of preferences in certain cases.	5. Application to be heard in Court.
50. Possession of property by trustee.	216. Debtor's books. 166. Annulment of composition. 247—249. Transfer of property and accounting. 259. No lien on debtor's books. 77, 78. Applications to commit.
51. Seizure of property of bankrupt.	75. To whom warrants addressed. 81—83. Duties of bailiff.
53. Appropriation of portion of pay or salary.	71—74. Appropriation of pay, &c. 11. Notice in writing. 19—29. Motions and practice.
54. Vesting and transfer of property.	166. On annulment of composition. 247—249. Transfer and accounting.

BANKRUPTCY ACT, 1883. SECT.	BANKRUPTCY RULES, 1883. RULE
55. Disclaimer	232. Of lease without leave.
57. Powers exerciseable by trustee with permission of committee of inspection.	225. Carrying on business. 91. Actions by trustees.
63. Declaration, distribution, &c. of dividends.	19—29. Motions and practice. 203—204. Gazetting. 175—177. Dividends. 199 (8). One dividend in small bankruptcies.
64. Power to allow bankrupt to manage property.	238. Subsistence allowance to debtor.
66. Appointment of official receivers.	233—259. Official receivers. 234. Appointment of deputy.
67. Deputy of official receiver ..	241, 242. Personal performance of duties and assistant.
68, 69, 70. Status and duties of official receiver.	117. Attestation of declaration of inability to pay. 127. Attestation of bankrupt's petition. 178. Certificate in application for discharge. 183. Proxies. 184 et seq. Meeting of creditors. 153. Advertisement of receiving order. 198—199. Small bankruptcies.
71. Power of Board of Trade to appoint officers.	241. Personal performance of duties.
72. Remuneration of trustee	224. Rate of remuneration.
73. Costs	98—110. Costs. 154. Costs of petition. 39. Prolixity. 94—96. Taxation of costs. 56, 57. Costs of witnesses. 67. Costs of mortgaged property.
74—81. Trustees, receipts, payments, accounts, audit, &c., &c.	228. Authority for account at local bank. 198, 199. Small bankruptcies. 207—217. Account and audit. 230. Copy of trustees' accounts. 251, 252. Payment into and out of bank. 225. Trustee carrying on bankrupt's business.
82. Release of trustee..........	226. Notice of application for release.
83. Official name of trustee	218—231. Trustees. 246, 247. Transfer of property from and account by official receiver to trustee.
84. Power to appoint joint or successive trustees.	Ditto.

BANKRUPTCY ACT, 1883.	BANKRUPTCY RULES, 1883.
SECT.	RULE
86. Removal of trustee	222. Removal of trustee. 227. Meeting to consider conduct.
89. Discretionary powers of trustee and control thereof.	175 et seq. Dividends. 186—190. Meetings of creditors. 229. Application to Court for directions.
90. Appeal to Court against trustee.	111—116. Appeals generally. 174. Proofs. 175 (3). Dividends.
91. Control of Board of Trade over trustees.	211. Board of Trade audit of trustees' accounts. 217. Annual returns.
92. The jurisdiction to be exercised by the High Court and County Courts.	88, 89. Sittings of County Courts. 90—97. Rules as to business of High Court.
94. Transaction of bankruptcy business by special judge of the High Court.	8—15. Proceedings generally. 79—83. Service and execution of process. 90—97. Rules relating to the business of the High Court.
95. Petition, where to be presented.	126. Place for filing petition. See notes to sect. 95 and rule 126.
97. Transfer of proceedings from Court to Court.	16—18. Transfer of proceedings.
98. Exercise in chambers of High Court jurisdiction.	5—7. Court and chambers.
99. Jurisdiction in bankruptcy of registrars.	*Passim* throughout the rules, and see especially 5—7. Court and chambers. 8—15. Proceedings. 16—18. Transfer of proceedings. 26, 27. Filing affidavits, &c. 32, 35, 37, 38. Security in Court. 243. Sudden emergency. 90—97. Business of High Court.
101. Board of Trade to make payments in accordance with the directions of the Court.	252. Payments out of Bank of England.
102. General powers of Bankruptcy Courts.	84—87. Trial by jury. 75—78. Warrants, arrests and commitments.
103. Judgment debtors	265—270. Rules under Debtors Act, 1869, s. 5, and sect. 103 of the Act.
104. Appeals in bankruptcy	111—116. Appeals. 174. Rejection or admission of proof. 175 (3). Dividends.

BANKRUPTCY ACT, 1883.	BANKRUPTCY RULES, 1883.
SECT.	RULE
105. Discretionary powers of Court.	53—63. Evidence by witnesses and depositions. 64. Discovery by interrogatories. 43—46, 49. Affidavits. 98 et seq. Costs. 84—87. Trial by jury. 124. Setting aside bankruptcy notice. 154. Costs of petition. 24. Adjournment. 260. Abridgment or extension of time, and see rr. 122 and 147.
109. Power to stay proceedings..	152. Stay of proceedings.
110—115. Sections as to partners, &c.	136. Several respondents. 192—197. Proceedings by or against firms. 215. Joint and separate estate accounts.
117. Enforcement of orders of Courts throughout the United Kingdom.	75 et seq. Warranty, arrests, commitments. 62. Disobedience to orders. 97. Execution of orders.
121. Summary administration in small bankruptcies.	198, 199. Small bankruptcies.
122. Power of County Court to make administration order instead of order for payment by instalments.	Special body of rules and forms of even date with the present rules, see p. 324, *post*.
125. Administration in bankruptcy of the estate of a person dying insolvent.	200—202. Administration of estate of person dying insolvent.
127. Power to make general rules.	Whole present body of rules, and see rr. 4 (1) Forms, and 257 Board of Trade Orders.
131. Returns by bankruptcy officers	205, 206. Book and returns, &c.
132. Gazette to be evidence	203, 204. Duty of Board of Trade. 15. Filing, Gazetting, &c. 153. Advertisement of receiving order. 157. Adjudication. 175. Dividend. 178—180. Discharge. 185. First meeting. 218, 219. Appointment of trustee. 222. Removal of trustee.
133, 134. Evidence of proceedings of meetings of creditors, and in bankruptcy.	8—15. As to proceedings. 190. Copy of resolution to be filed. 207. Record book.
135. Swearing of affidavits	39—50. Affidavits.
136. Death of witness	58. Depositions, &c.

BANKRUPTCY ACT, 1883.	BANKRUPTCY RULES, 1883.
SECT.	RULE
137. Bankruptcy Courts to have seals.	12. Process to be sealed.
138. Certificate of appointment of trustee.	218, 219. Form of certificate, &c. 203, 204. Gazetting. 15. Filing.
141. Computation of time	3. Computation of time.
142. Service of notices	25. Personal service. 35. Notice of sureties. 38. Notice of deposit. 54, 55. Service of subpœnas. 71, 72. Notices as to appropriation of pay. 78. Notice of application to commit. 79—83. Service and execution of process. 114. Notice of appeal. 122. Service of bankruptcy notice. 144—148. Service of creditor's petition. 153. Notice as to receiving order. 157. Notice of adjudication. 160. Notice of application for approval of composition. 175. Notice of dividend. 180. Notice of discharge. 184. Notice to debtor of meeting of creditors. 193. Service on firm. 201. Service of petition under sect. 125. 223. Notice of resignation.
143. Formal defects not to invalidate proceedings.	46. Formal defects. 118 (3). Wrong Court.
144. Exemption of deeds from stamp duty.	51—52. Stamps.
148. Acting of corporations, partners, &c.	191. Proceedings by company, partnership.
149. Construction of Acts mentioning commission of bankruptcy, &c.	263. Saving for existing laws.
151. Saving of existing rights of audience.	29. Precedence of motions.
159, 160. Transfer of estates, outstanding property, &c., on vacancy of office under the Bankruptcy Act, 1869.	264. Pending proceedings.
162. Unclaimed and undistributed dividends and funds under this and former Acts.	255, 256. Unclaimed funds, &c.

BANKRUPTCY ACT, 1883.	BANKRUPTCY RULES, 1883.
SECT.	RULE
168. Interpretation of terms	2. Interpretation of terms.
169. Repeal of enactments and previous proceedings.	263. Saving for existing laws. 264. Pending proceedings.
170. Proceedings under sects. 125 and 126 of the Bankruptcy Act, 1869.	264. Pending proceedings.
Schedule.	
I. Meetings of creditors	183. Proxies and voting papers. 184—190. Meeting of creditors.
II. Proof of debts	169—174. Proof of debts. 39—50. Affidavits. 84—88. Trial by jury. 5 (g). Matters to be heard in Court; and see 19—29. Motions and practice.

RULES UNDER SECTIONS 127 AND 122.

THE Rules after the preliminary portion, dealing with title, interpretation, &c. are divided into five parts:—

PART I.—Court procedure. (Rules 5—116.)

    II.—Proceedings from act of bankruptcy to discharge. (Rules 117—197.)

    III.—Special procedures (under which are included small bankruptcies and the administration of estates of persons dying insolvent). (Rules 198—202.)

    IV.—Officers, trustees, audit, &c. (Rules 203—256.)

    V.—Miscellaneous matters (Rules 257—264), and Rules under sect. 5 of the Debtors Act, 1869, and sect. 103 of the Act. (Rules 265—270.) These Rules are followed by the Appendix of Forms—128 in number, which are referred to in the body of the Rules.

A separate body of Rules and Forms has also been issued under sect. 122, see *post*, p. 324.

THE BANKRUPTCY RULES, 1883,

UNDER SECT. 127.

Preliminary. RULES 1—3.

THE first three Rules, dealing with the short title, the date of the commencement of the Rules, the interpretation of terms and computation of time, are to be read in conjunction with sect. 1 (short title), p. 1; sect. 3 (commencement of Act), p. 2; sect. 141 (computation of time), p. 206; and sect. 168 (interpretation of terms), p. 231.

Rule 2. See sect. 168 of the Act, p. 231.

"The Court," which is there defined as the Court having jurisdiction in bankruptcy under the Act, is by this rule to be read as including the registrar of such Court.

"Trustee" includes official receiver when acting as trustee. See as to official receiver, sect. 68 (3), p. 131, and note to sect. 66, p. 129.

Forms. RULE 4.

Rule 4, as to the employment of the forms in the Appendix, corresponds to the provisions contained in the Rules of the Supreme Court, 1883, Ord. XIX. rr. 2, 5.

(2) See as to the functions of the Board of Trade being of an administrative and not of a judicial order, Introduction, pp. xlv *et seq.*, and notes to sect. 101, p. 166.

Compare the analogous power of the masters under the Rules of the Supreme Court, 1883, Ord. LXI. r. 33, as to prescribing the use of modified or additional forms.

Part I.—Court Procedure.

Court and Chambers. RULES 5—7.

The three Rules dealing with the matters to be heard in Court, the jurisdiction of the registrars and adjournments from chambers to Court, and *vice versâ*, are to be read in conjunction with the various sections, which will be found cited on the next page.

Rule 5 introduces a most important change as to the conduct of business.

The only matters which could not be disposed of in chambers, under the Rules of 1870 (Rule 5), was the public examination of the debtor and the granting of an order of discharge.

Rules 5, 6 and 7 now provide that "the following "matters and applications shall be heard and deter- "mined in open Court, namely :—

" (a) The public examination of debtors ;

" (b) Application to approve a composition or scheme "of arrangement ;

" (c) Applications for orders of discharge or certifi- "cates of removal of disqualifications ;

" (d) Appeals from the Board of Trade to the High "Court ;

" (e) Applications to set aside or avoid any settle- "ment, conveyance, transfer, security or "payment, or to declare for or against the "title of the trustee to any property ad- "versely claimed ;

" (f) Applications for the committal of any person "to prison for contempt ;

" (g) Appeals against the rejection of a proof, or "applications to expunge or reduce a proof, "where the amount of the proof exceeds "200*l.* ;

" (h) Applications for the trial of issues of fact with "a jury, and the trial of such issues.

" Any other matter or application may be heard and "determined in chambers.

" 6. A registrar may, under the general or special
" directions of the judge, hear and determine any
" matter or application mentioned in sub-sect. (2) of
" sect. 99 of the Act.

" 7. Subject to the provisions of the Act and these
" Rules, any matter or application may, at any time, if
" the judge (or, as the case may be, the registrar) thinks
" fit, be adjourned from chambers to Court or from Court
" to chambers; and if all the contending parties require
" any matter or application to be adjourned from cham-
" bers into Court it should be so adjourned."

Rule 5.—(a) See, as to public examination, sect. 17,
p. 27.

(b) See, as to approval of compositions and schemes
of arrangement, sect. 18 (4), p. 30; sect. 23 (1 and 2),
p. 43.

(c) See, as to orders of discharge, sect. 28, p. 53;
and as to certificates of removal of disabilities, sect.
32 (2), p. 63.

(d) See, as to appeals from the Board of Trade, note
to sect. 104, p. 177.

(e) See, as to avoidance of settlement, &c., sect. 47,
p. 99; sect. 48, p. 101; and as to trustee's title, sects. 43
et seq., pp. 89 *et seq.*

(f) See, as to applications for committal, sect. 102 (5),
p. 169.

(g) See, as to proof, &c., sect. 37, p. 69, and
Schedule II. (22—27), p. 245.

(h) See, as to applications for the trial of issues,
sect. 102 (3), p. 167.

Rule 6. Note that the jurisdiction conferred upon
the registrar by sect. 99 (p. 165) is limited by the fact
that there must be a general or special direction of a
judge.

Rule 7. See, as to jurisdiction at chambers, sect. 98,
p. 163.   Note, here, that the judge or registrar has a
discretionary power as to adjournment from or to
chambers; but that the power "*shall*" be exercised if
all the contending parties join in requiring it.

Proceedings. RULES 8—15.

The eight Rules dealing with the question of proceedings are to be read in conjunction with sects. 92 *et seq.* (as to constitution, procedure and powers of Court), pp. 159 *et seq.*; sect. 132 (evidence), p. 202; sect. 137 (Bankruptcy Court to have seals), p. 205; and Sched. I. r. 5, p. 237.

Rule 8 provides, with regard to the title, &c. of proceedings, that—

"(1) Every proceeding in Court under the Act shall " be dated, and shall be intituled 'In Bankruptcy,' and " with the name of the Court in which it is taken, and " of the matter to which it relates. Numbers and dates " may be denoted by figures.

"(2) All applications and orders shall be intituled " *ex parte* the applicant.

"(3) The first proceeding in every matter shall have " a distinctive number assigned to it by the registrar, " and all subsequent proceedings in the same matter shall " bear the same number.

"(4) When a matter is transferred from one Court " to another it shall receive a new distinctive number."

Rule 9 corresponds with Rule 8 of the General Rules of 1870, except that parchment is no longer mentioned; the Rule now applies to all proceedings, while notices to creditors were excepted in the Rules of 1870. Rules 10, 12, 13 and 14 are substantially Rules 9, 10, 11 and 12 of the Rules of 1870. By Rule 11 all notices required by the Act or Rules, unless otherwise provided by the Rules, or ordered by the Court in any particular case, are to be in writing. By Rule 15 every registrar "of each Court" (*i. e.*, we presume each Court having jurisdiction in bankruptcy) is to file a copy of each issue of the "Gazette," and of each local paper in which an advertisement appears, and is to file memoranda of the advertisement, which are to be *primâ facie* evidence of their insertion, along with the proceedings. (See an article in the Solicitors' Journal, vol. 27, p. 594, on the difficulty which arose sometime ago in *The Queen* v. *Lowe*.)

Transfer of Proceedings. RULES 16—18.

These three Rules, dealing with the transfer of proceedings, are to be read in conjunction with sect. 97 (transfer of proceedings from Court to Court), p. 162.

The Rules themselves correspond substantially with Rules 82—84 of the Rules of 1870, except that the power of certifying for transfer, which, under the former Rules, was only conferred upon the County Court judge, is now given also to the judge or a registrar of the High Court.

Rule 17 corresponds with Rule 83 of the Rules of 1870, except that the words "within seven days after " the first meeting, or, in any other case," are new.

Motions and Practice. RULES 19—29.

These Rules correspond, with some material alterations and slight differences as to mode of sub-division, with Rules 50 *et seq.* of the Rules of 1870.

The following are the material alterations :—

1. The Court is now expressly empowered by Rule 20, which corresponds with Rules of the Supreme Court, Ord. LII. r. 3, to make orders on *ex parte* applications.

2. The length of the notice of motion is altered from four clear days to eight days.

Rule 29 (precedence of motions) provides—

"Except in cases of emergency, or for any other " cause deemed sufficient by the Court, all motions shall " be made and heard in the order in which they are " set down at the sitting of the Court."

The words in the original draft of the Rules, preserving the precedence of counsel, as in Rule 57 of the Rules of 1870, was struck out.

Security in Court. RULES 30—38.

The following nine Rules, dealing with the question of security in Court, are to be read in conjunction with sect. 7 (5), p. 14 (as to petitioner giving security); sect. 36, p. 68 (as to giving bond security in Court in respect of disputed debt), but must be distinguished from the security given by trustee or special manager dealt with by Rule 252.

Affidavits.   RULES 39—50.

The twelve Rules dealing with the subject of affidavits are to be read in conjunction with sect. 135 of the Act, p. 203, as to swearing of affidavits, and are taken to some slight extent from the Bankruptcy Rules, 1870, but almost entirely from the Rules of the Supreme Court, 1883, Ord. XXXVIII., the object being to assimilate the practice in bankruptcy to that in the High Court, with which the Court of Bankruptcy is now consolidated.   (Sect. 93, p. 158.)   Note, however, that the proviso in Ord. XXXVIII. r. 7, that affidavits are to be written or printed bookwise, is here omitted.

Rules 39 and 40 ought to be carefully noted, as they introduce stringent regulations as to the costs of affidavits which are not in the proper form.

Rule 40 is identical with the Rules of the Supreme Court, 1883, Ord. XXXVIII. r. 7, except that in the latter Rule, every affidavit, whether written or printed, is to be made bookwise.   The practice in bankruptcy is in this respect unaltered.

Rule 43.   See, as to striking out scandalous matter, *Christie* v. *Christie*, L. R., 8 Ch. 499; *Coyle* v. *Cuming*, 27 W. R. 529; *Millington* v. *Loring*, 6 Q. B. D. 190.   The Court can act with regard to scandalous matter, not only on the application of the aggrieved party, but also on the application of any party interested, or without any application at all.   (*Cracknell* v. *Janson*, 11 Ch. D. 1.)

"The sole question in such a case is whether the matter alleged to be scandalous has a tendency, or, in other words, would be admissible in evidence to show the truth of any allegation that is material.   Our law does not allow you to prove that a man has a bad character for the purpose of showing that because he has a bad character it is probable that he will have committed a certain crime." (Per Lord Selborne and Mellish, L. J.,

Christie v. *Christie, ubi. supra,* where the question of costs is discussed, and the principle laid down to be that the offending party must pay to the other parties the whole expense to which they have been put by his introduction of libellous matter.)

Rule 44 is substantially the same as the Rules of the Supreme Court, 1883, Ord. XXXVIII. r. 12, subject to the omission of the words " or if taken at the " central office, either by his initials or by the stamps of " that office."

Rule 48 is identical with the Rules of the Supreme Court, 1883, Ord. XXXVIII. rr. 16 and 17, with the exception of the words " other than a proof."

Rule 50 provides, with regard to the proof of affidavits, that the Court shall take judicial notice of the seal or signature of any person authorized by or under the Act to take affidavits, or to certify to such authority.

Stamps. RULES 51, 52.

These two Rules, dealing with the question of stamps, are to be read in conjunction with sect. 144 of the Act.

Rule 51 corresponds precisely with Rule 206 of the General Rules of 1870 ; while Rule 52 extends the definition of bankruptcy and bankrupt so as to include for the purposes of sect. 144 all proceedings under the Act.

Witnesses and Depositions. RULES 53—63.

The eleven Rules dealing with the subject of witnesses and depositions are to be read in conjunction with sect. 27 (discovery of debtors' property), p. 50, and see note, p. 52 ; sect. 99 (h) (registrar's powers), p. 164 ; sect. 105 (5) (procedure), p. 178 ; sect. 136 (death of witness), p. 204.

Rule 53 corresponds with Rule 166 of the Rules of 1870 (with the necessary addition as to the official receiver), except that according to the present rule the names of three witnesses may be inserted in the subpœna.

The next Rule settles the practice as to service in accordance with the decision in *Re Lancaster, Ex parte Lancaster*, 3 Ch. Div. 498.

Rule 59 corresponds to a considerable extent with Rule 207 of the General Rules of 1870, except that the words " at any stage of the proceedings " and " a person other than the person before whom the examination is taken " are new. The rate of remuneration is also altered from one guinea per day to three shillings and sixpence per hour, and for the transcript fourpence per folio of seventy-two words instead of eightpence for ninety words.

Rules 55, 56, 57 correspond with Rules 168, 169, 170 of the Rules of 1870.

Rules 58, 60, 61, 62, 63, are taken from the Rules of the Supreme Court, 1883, Ord. XXXVII. rr. 5, 6, 7, 8, 9.

<h2 style="text-align:center">Discovery. RULE 64.</h2>

This Rule, dealing with the question of discovery generally, is to be read, so far as circumstances admit, in conjunction with the Rules of the Supreme Court, 1883, Ord. XXXI. Applications under it are to be made *ex parte*.

Taking Accounts of Property Mortgaged, and of the Sale thereof. RULES 65—69.

These five Rules correspond with Rules 78—81 of the Rules of 1870, except that the present Rules deal only with mortgages over real or leasehold estate, while the terms of the Rules of 1870 were more extensive, as (1) they spoke not only of mortgages but also of securities, and (2) as to " any estate or effects whether real or personal," while the present Rules speak only of real or leasehold estate. The words " if satisfied that there ought to be a sale," which must render satisfying the Court on this point a condition precedent before the notice is to be given, are new. The latter part of Rule 65, enabling the mortgagee to bid and purchase at any such sale, and Rule 69, empowering the Court to order all accounts, &c., as in the Chancery Division, are also new.

Discovery of Debtor's Property.   RULE 70.

This Rule is to be read in conjunction with sect. 27 (discovery of debtor's property) of the Act, p. 50. It is the same as Rule 170 of the Rules of 1870, with the addition of the official receiver and Board of Trade.

Appropriation of Pay, Salary, Pension, &c.
RULES 71—74.

The following four Rules, dealing with the question of the appropriation of pay, salary or pension of a bankrupt, are to be read in conjunction with sect. 53 (appropriation of pay or salary of a debtor), p. 109 ; and Rule 74 (as to review of the order) with sect. 104 (appeals in bankruptcy), p. 173, of the Act.

These Rules correspond with Rules 180 to 182 of the Rules of 1870, except that Rule 72, requiring that a copy of the proposed order should be sent to the chief of the department before an application under sect. 53 (1) (see note thereon, p. 110), can be made, is new.

Warrants, Arrests and Commitments.
RULES 75—78.

The following four Rules, dealing with warrants, arrests and commitments, are to be read in conjunction with sect. 25 (as to arrest of debtor), p. 47 ; sect. 27 (2) (discovery of debtor's property), p. 50 ; sect. 51 (as to seizure of property of bankrupt), p. 107 ; sect. 103 (as to judgment debtors), p. 169 ; and sects. 117—120 (as to orders and warrants of Court), pp. 185—187, of the Act. They correspond substantially with the Rules 176—180 of the General Rules of 1870.

Service and Execution of Process.
RULES 79—83.

The following five Rules, dealing with the question of service and the execution of process, are to be read in conjunction with sect. 7 (2) (proceedings and order on creditor's petition), p. 13; sect. 11 (service of order staying proceedings), p. 21; sect. 46 (duties of sheriff as to goods taken in execution), p. 98; sect. 142 (service of notices), p. 207; and Sched. II. rule 2 (proof of debts), p. 241.

Rule 79 substantially corresponds with the Rules of the Supreme Court, 1883, Ord. IV. rr. 1 and 4, except that the provision in case one solicitor acts as agent for another is here omitted, probably because such matters in bankruptcy would be generally transacted in the County Courts.

Rule 80 is substantially the same as Rules of the Supreme Court, 1883, Ord. LXIV. r. 11.

Rule 81 corresponds to a great extent with Rule 58 of the Rules of 1870; but the latter part provides that this Rule shall not be construed to require any order, summons, petition or notice to be served by a bailiff or officer of the Court, unless the Court shall so direct.

Rule 82 provides that notices which may be served by post shall be sent by registered letter. By Rule 83, every order of the Court may be enforced as if it were a judgment of the Court to the same effect.

Trial by Jury. RULES 84—87.

The following four Rules, dealing with the question of trial by jury, are to be read with sect. 102 (general power of Bankruptcy Courts), p. 166, of the Act.

Rule 84 is identical with Rule 190 of the Rules of 1870. It is to be observed, that as the practice is now settled (Rule 86) by reference to that in the County Courts and Queen's Bench Division, the bulk of the former Rules specifying the practice of the Bankruptcy Court as to trial by jury are here omitted. See as to mode of trial, the Rules of the Supreme Court, 1883, Ord. XXXVI; and as to County Courts, Pitt-Lewis's County Court Practice, Chaps. XIII. and XIV.

Rule 87 provides, that when the issues of fact are tried in the Queen's Bench Division otherwise than before the special judge assigned for bankruptcy business, the verdict or finding is to be endorsed on the record for trial, and returned to the senior bankruptcy registrar of the High Court. *Semble*, a motion for a new trial will be to the Divisional Court.

Sittings of County Court. RULES 88, 89.

The following two Rules, dealing with the sittings of a County Court, are to be read in conjunction with sect. 92 (jurisdiction to be exercised by High Court and County Courts), p. 156; sect. 95 (petition, where to be presented), p. 160; sect. 97 (transfer of proceedings from Court to Court), p. 162; sect. 99 (jurisdiction in bankruptcy of registrar), p. 163; sect. 100 (powers of County Court), p. 165; sect. 103 (3) (judgment debtor's summons to be bankruptcy business), p. 170; sect. 104 (appeals in bankruptcy), p. 173; sect. 105 (discretionary powers of the Court), p. 177; sect. 122 (power of County Court to make administration order instead of order for payment by instalments), p. 189; sect. 125 (administration in bankruptcy of estate of person dying insolvent), p. 194, of the Act.

Note that by the latter part of Rule 89, special appointments for bankruptcy business are not to interfere with the determination of any such business in the general course.

Rules relating to the Business of the High Court. RULES 90—97.

The following eight Rules, which relate to the business of the High Court, are to be read in conjunction with sect. 94 (transaction of bankruptcy business by special judge of High Court), p. 159; sect. 57 (powers exerciseable by trustee with permission of committee of inspection), p. 121; sect. 113 (action by trustee and bankrupt's partners), p. 182, of the Act.

Rules 90, 92, 93, 94, 95, 96 substantially correspond with Rules 209, 211, 214, 223, 224, 225, with only such modifications as are necessitated by the fact that the Bankruptcy Court is now (by sect. 92, p. 156) consolidated with the High Court.

With regard to actions by trustees, Rule 91 provides that—

"When a trustee, under sect. 57 of the Act, brings " an action in the High Court concerning any matter " not specially assigned by the Supreme Court of Judi- " cature Act, 1873, or Acts amending it or by Rules of " the Supreme Court, to a Division other than that to " which bankruptcy business is assigned, he shall bring " his action in the Division to which bankruptcy busi- " ness is assigned, and the action shall, unless the Court " otherwise directs, be tried by the judge assigned to " transact and dispose of bankruptcy business."

With regard to the execution of orders, Rule 97 provides that—

"Writs of execution shall issue from the proper " department of the Central Office, and all proceedings " thereon and in relation thereto shall be regulated as " nearly as may be by the Rules of the Supreme Court " for the time being in force in relation to execution."

Costs. RULES 98—110.

The following thirteen Rules, dealing with the subject of costs, are to be read in conjunction with sect. 73 (costs), p. 138; and sect. 105 (discretionary powers of the Court), p. 177, of the Act.

Rules 99, 100 and 101 substantially correspond with Rules 187, 188, 189 of the Rules of 1870. The changes effected by the other portion of the Rules on this important subject are of an extremely important character.

Rule 98 enables the Court to award costs in four different ways—(1) as between party and party; (2) as between solicitor and client; (3) full costs, charges and expenses; or (4) the Court may fix a sum to be paid in lieu of taxed costs.

Sub-sect. 2 provides, that "in the absence of any "express direction costs of an opposed motion shall "follow the event and shall be taxed as between party "and party."

Rule 102 provides that in County Courts costs shall be taxed by the registrar in person.

Rule 103 prescribes the cases which the lower scale of costs is to apply. It is to be observed that the lower scale of costs is the same as that under the General Rules of 1871, viz., three-fifths of the ordinary charges, *plus* disbursements; but that, while under the Rules of 1871, this scale was to be adopted if the provable debts did not exceed 750*l.* or the estimated assets 200*l.*, now the sole test is estimated assets not exceeding 300*l.* A second noteworthy point is that the lesser scale did not apply to compositions (*Ex parte Castle, Re Meikle,* 1 Ch. D. 111), while now it applies to all proceedings in bankruptcy.

Rule 104 enables the Board of Trade to require the taxation of bill of costs, &c. of any solicitor, accountant, auctioneer, manager or other person which has been made by a registrar of a County Court, to be reviewed by a Bankruptcy Taxing Master of the High Court. It is to be observed that no rule is laid down as to how the costs of such taxation beyond the costs of the appearance of the person whose bill is taxed are to be borne.

Rule 105. The order of payment of costs incurred under a bankruptcy petition prior to the first meeting of creditors are dealt with by the next Rule (105). The order of priority, in the absence of express direction, is to be—(1) Ad valorem duty; (2) expenses of realization; (3) fees payable to officers of the Court; (4) remuneration of special manager; (5) taxed costs of the petitioner; (6) charges of any person duly appointed to assist the debtor in the preparation of his statement of affairs. Attention may here be directed to the very important provisions as to costs contained in Rule 154, which will be found at length, *post*, p. 310.

Rule 106 obliges the solicitor, where a debtor has presented a petition against himself, to give credit in his bill of costs for any deposit he may have received.

Rule 107, like Rule 113 of the Rules of 1870, enables the Court to order costs of joint estate to be paid out of separate estate, and *vice versâ*.

By Rule 108, the taxing master is to make a special note upon the allocatur when costs are to be paid otherwise than out of the estate of the bankrupt; while by Rules 109, 110, a file and register are to be kept of all bills taxed.

Appeals. RULES 111—116.

The following six Rules, dealing with the question of appeals, are to be read in conjunction with sect. 104 (appeals in bankruptcy) of the Act, and the note thereon, in which the subject is fully dealt with, and the various sections of the Act under which any appeal is given, pp. 173—177, collated.

The right of appeal is now restricted in three cases.

Rule 111 provides that, " (1) Except by leave of the " Court, there shall be no appeal to the Court of Appeal " from any order made by consent, or as to costs only.

" (2) No appeal to the Court of Appeal shall be " brought from any order relating to property when it " is apparent from the proceedings that the money or " money's worth involved does not exceed 50*l.*, unless " by leave of the Court.

" (3) No appeal shall be brought in respect of the " omission by the Court appealed from to exercise any " discretionary power, unless the Court shall in its " judgment, or on application made at the hearing, have " expressly refused to exercise such power, in which " case the refusal may be made a ground of appeal."

Sub-sect. 1 is taken with some modification from the Supreme Court of Judicature Act, 1873, sect. 49.

It is to be observed that in the first two sub-sections (which speak only of appeals to the Court of Appeal) there may be an appeal by leave, but in the third there is no such exception.

Rule 112. The provision as to time for appeal, twenty-one days from perfection of order or refusal, is the same as that contained in the Rules of the Supreme Court, 1883, Ord. LXIII. r. 15.

Rule 113. The principle upon which the amount of security is fixed by the Court is not the value of the property involved; the Court "rather considers the probable costs of the appeal." (Per Cotton, L.J., *Morecroft* v. *Evans*, W. N. 1882, p. 189.)

Semble, the former practice laid down in *Ex parte Rosenthal* (20 Ch. Div. 315), *Ex parte Luxon* (20 Ch. Div. 701), will still prevail, *i. e.*, that before entering an appeal in bankruptcy, the registrar ought to give a direction to the Bank of England to receive the deposit payable on the entry, and not to enter the appeal until he receives from the Bank a certificate that the money has been paid, applies to appeals from the chief judge to the Court of Appeal. *Semble*, however, "at or before" would be construed as equivalent to "about," and the payment would be in time if made at the earliest possible moment after the entry of the appeal. (Per Jessel, M.R., 20 Ch. Div. 319.)

Semble, see as to motion for new trial, *ante*, p. 301.

Part II.— Proceedings from Act of Bankruptcy to Discharge.

Declaration of Inability to Pay Debts. RULE 117.

This Rule, dealing with the question of declaration of inability to pay debts, is to be read in conjunction with sect. 4 (acts of bankruptcy), p. 3, of the Act.

The declaration must be attested by one of the following persons:—(1) Solicitor; (2) Justice of the Peace; (3) Official Receiver; (4) Registrar of the Court.

Bankruptcy Notice.   RULES 118—124.

The seven Rules dealing with this important novelty in bankruptcy law are to be read in conjunction with sect. 4 (acts of bankruptcy), pp. 3, 10.

The provisions are, to a considerable extent, the same as those in the Rules of 1870 (17—25) with regard to the abolished debtor's summons, which is now superseded by the bankruptcy notice. (See p. 10.)

By Rule 120, the bankruptcy notice must have an endorsement giving the debtor notice that under proper circumstances he may file an affidavit setting up a counter-claim, set-off, or cross-demand, which is to have the effect of an application to set aside the notice.

The time within which the affidavit must be filed is, in the case of a notice served in England, three days, Rule 120 (3). The notice itself must be served within a month, and by Rule 124, when the Court makes an order setting aside the bankruptcy notice, it may at the same time declare that no act of bankruptcy has been committed under it.

Bankruptcy Petition.   RULES 125—128.

The four Rules dealing with the question of a bankruptcy petition are to be read in conjunction with sect. 5 (jurisdiction to make receiving order), p. 11 ; sect. 6 (conditions on which creditor may petition), p. 11; sect. 7 (proceedings and order on creditor's petition), p. 13 ; sect. 8 (debtor's petition and order thereon), p. 18 ; sect. 68 (2) (status of official receiver), p. 131; sect. 95 (petition, where to be presented), p. 160 ; sect. 106 et seq. (consolidation of petitions), pp. 179 et seq. ; sect. 121 (summary administration in small cases), p. 187 ; sect. 125 (administration in bankruptcy of estate of person dying insolvent), p. 194.

Rule 125 substantially corresponds with sect. 27 of the Bankruptcy Act, 1870. The provisions as to lodging two copies appears only to apply to creditors' petitions. (Rule 131, *post*.)

Rule 126 contemplates a case not provided for by sect. 95

of the Act (and see note thereon, p. 161), viz. where the
debtor has carried on business in one district and
resided in another.

The bankruptcy petition, if attested in England,
must be attested in the same way as the declaration of
inability to pay debts, viz., by (1) a solicitor, or (2) a
justice of the peace, or (3) an official receiver, or
(4) a registrar of the Court ; if attested out of England,
it must be attested before a judge or magistrate, or a
British consul or vice-consul, or a notary public.

Rule 128 requires the petitioner, whether he be the
debtor himself, or a creditor, to deposit 5l. and such
further sum as the Court may direct, which is to be ac-
counted for by the official receiver, and repaid out of
the first net proceeds of the estate.

Creditor's Petition. RULES 129—143.

The following fifteen Rules, dealing with a creditor's
petition and the procedure thereunder, are to be read
in conjunction with sect. 6 (conditions on which
creditor may petition), p. 11; sect. 7 (proceedings and
order on creditor's petition), p. 13; sect. 10 (discretionary powers as to appointment of receiver and stay
of proceedings), p. 20; sect. 11. (power to dismiss
petition against some respondents only), p. 181;
sect. 109 (power to stay proceedings), p. 181; sect. 102
(general power of bankruptcy Courts), p. 166; sect. 121
(summary administration in small cases), p. 187;
sect. 125 (administration in bankruptcy of estate of
person dying insolvent), p. 194.

Rule 129 contains a new provision, enabling the
Court to order security for costs in four cases, viz., when
the petitioning creditor is (1) resident abroad, or
(2) bankrupt, &c., or (3) when a petition is pending
against him under this Act, or (4) when he has made
default in payment of any costs ordered by any Court
to be paid by him to the debtor.

Rules 131, 133, 135, 136, 139, 140, 141, 143, are substantially the same as Rules 29, 32, 34, 35, 38, 39, 40, 44 respectively, of the Rules of 1870.

Rule 134 extends the right of application for the appointment of an interim receiver and manager (now the official receiver) under Rule 33 of the Rules of 1870, " to the debtor himself," but imposes a new condition on the applicant upon which the Court may make the order, viz. " upon such terms as to deposit for expenses and otherwise as may seem just." The new Rule, unlike the old, appears to contemplate cases where the costs of the interim receiver and manager may not be thrown on the petitioner.

Rules 137 and 142 correspond with Rules 36 and 43 of the Rules of 1870, except that the present Rules require service of the notice on the solicitors or solicitor, if known, as well as the parties.

By Rule 138 the Court is to have such proof of the statements in the petition as it shall think sufficient; under Rule 37 of the Rules of 1870 an adjudication might be made without further proof than the statements in the petition.

Service of Creditors' Petition. RULES 144—148.

The five Rules dealing with the question of service of a creditor's petition are to be read in conjunction with sect. 7 (proceedings and order on creditor's petition), p. 13; sect. 100 (powers of County Courts), p. 165; sect. 105 (discretionary powers of the Court), p. 177.

Rules 146, 147, 148 substantially correspond with Rules 63, 64, 66 respectively of the Rules of 1870, with the exception that the words in Rule 66, "upon such evidence as shall satisfy it that the service will be effectual or sufficient," are now omitted.

Rule 144, as to personal service of petition, corresponds with Rule 60 of the Rules of 1870, except that the words in the latter Rule "seven days before the day of its hearing," are now omitted.

Rule 145 as to substituted service corresponds with Rule 61 of the Rules of 1870; service may now be effected by some person in the employ of the persons mentioned in the Rule, which has the effect of giving a legislative sanction to the law as stated in *Re Lancaster*, 3 Ch. D. 498.

Hearing of Petition. RULE 149.

This Rule, dealing with the hearing of the petition, is to be read in conjunction with sect. 7 (proceedings and order on creditor's petition), p. 13; sect. 8 (debtor's petition and order thereon), p. 18; sect. 99 (jurisdiction in bankruptcy of registrar), p. 163; sect. 98 (exercise in chambers of High Court jurisdiction), p. 163; sect. 105 (discretionary powers of the Court), p. 177; sect. 106 (consolidation of petitions), p. 179; sect. 109 (power to stay proceedings), p. 181; sect. 111 (power to dismiss petition against some respondents only), p. 181.

By Rule 149, in the case of a debtor's petition the receiving order is to be made forthwith. A creditor's petition, on the other hand, is not to be heard until the expiration of eight days after service, but the Court has a discretionary power to hear it sooner under any of the following circumstances:—

1. When the debtor has filed a declaration of inability to pay his debts;
2. On satisfactory proof that the debtor has absconded;
3. In any other case for good cause shown.

Receiving Orders. RULES 150—154.

The following five Rules, dealing with the subject of receiving orders, are to be read in conjunction with sect. 5 (jurisdiction to make receiving order), p. 11; sect. 7 (proceedings and order on creditor's petition), p. 13; sect. 8 (debtor's petition and order thereon), p. 18; sect. 9—11 (effect of receiving order), pp. 19—21; sect. 103 (judgment debtor's summons to be bankruptcy business), p. 169; sect. 142 (service of notices) p. 207; sect. 73 (allowance and taxation of costs), p. 138; sect. 105 (discretionary powers of the Court), p. 177.

Several important details are here supplied by the Rules. The Court, at the same time when it makes a receiving order, *shall* fix a day for the public examination of the debtor (and note that by Rule 155 the debtor may then be made a bankrupt on his own application), and the receiving order may include a particular or general stay of proceedings.

Rule 151 prescribes three cases in which a receiving order is not to be made on a bankruptcy notice, viz.— (1) where the debtor has applied to set aside the notice until after the hearing of such application; or (2) where the notice has been set aside; or (3) during a stay of proceedings.

Rule 153 deals with the question of the advertisement of the receiving order.

Rule 154 contains an extremely important provision with regard to costs. The line of demarcation is fixed after the receiving order. All costs up to that point are to be borne by the party prosecuting the proceedings; but "when once the receiving order is made, the Court "may make an order for the payment of the costs of "the petitioning creditor (including the costs of the "bankruptcy notice (if any) sued out by him) out of "the first net proceeds of the estate, and a com- "position or scheme which does not provide for the "payment in full of any costs so awarded may be "disallowed.

"When the proceeds of the estate are not sufficient "for the payment of any costs necessarily incurred by "the official receiver (in excess of the deposit) between "the making of a receiving order and the conclusion of "the first meeting of creditors, the Court may order "such costs to be paid by the party prosecuting the pro- "ceedings."

Adjudication. RULES 155—158.

The following four Rules, dealing with the question of adjudication, are to be read in conjunction with sect. 20 (adjudication of bankruptcy where composition not accepted or approved), p. 37; sect. 18 (11) (power for creditors to accept and Court to approve composition or arrangement), p. 31; sect. 23 (3) (power to accept composition or scheme after bankruptcy adjudication), p. 41; sect. 132 (Gazette to be evidence), p. 202; sect. 35 (power of Court to annul adjudication in certain cases), p. 67.

An important point is here introduced, viz. enabling the Court to adjudge the debtor bankrupt on his own application.

Rule 156 supplements sect. 20 (see note, p. 37), by prescribing five additional sets of circumstances under which the Court may, either on the application of a creditor or of the official receiver, make an immediate adjudication in bankruptcy; but note, that under the circumstances mentioned in the Rule the power is discretionary and to be exercised on the application of a creditor or of the official receiver, while under sect. 20 of the Act it is obligatory.

Rules 157 and 158 deal with the Gazetting, &c. of the order of adjudication and of its annulment.

Composition or Scheme under Sections 18 or 23.

RULES 159—167.

The nine Rules dealing with compositions or schemes of arrangement are to be read in conjunction with sect. 18 (power for creditors to accept and Court to approve composition or arrangement), p. 29; sect. 23 (power to accept composition or scheme after bankruptcy adjudication), p. 43, of the Act.

A number of important points are supplied by the Rules.

The terms of the composition or scheme are to be settled at the first meeting or adjournments thereof. (Rule 159.)

At the second meeting, should the composition or scheme be rejected, the meeting may proceed to appoint a trustee, *i. e.*, *semble* in the bankruptcy of the debtor. (*Ibid.*)

The subsequent Rules, 160—163, deal with the notice of the application which is to be given (seven days), the evidence by which it must be supported, and the order to be made thereon, which is to be Gazetted by the Board of Trade.

Formal slips may be corrected by the Court, but no alteration in substance may be made.

The subsequent Rules, 163—166, appear to contemplate the distinction pointed out at p. 33, between cases where there is a *cessio bonorum*, and those in which the property still remains in the debtor.

No action can now be brought for non-payment of the composition, but the only remedy is by application to the Court.   See note at p. 35, and note that the effect is to assimilate the law as to compositions with that in bankruptcy under sect. 63 of the present Act, and that in compositions under sect. 126 of the Act of 1869.

Rule 167 makes provision in case of disputed claims as to securing the amount until the determination of the dispute.

Statement of Affairs. Rule 168.

This Rule, dealing with the debtor's statement of affairs, is to be read in conjunction with sect. 16 (debtor's statement of affairs), p. 24; sect. 70 (duties of official receiver as to debtor's estate), p. 133, and Rules 237 and 239.

Proof of Debts. Rules 169—174.

The following six Rules, dealing with the question of proof of debts, are to be read in conjunction with sect. 37 (description of debts provable in bankruptcy), p. 69; Sched. II. (proof of debts), p. 241; sect. 54 (vesting and transfer of property), p. 111.

By Rule 170 one clear day is the time within which proofs must be lodged with the official receiver, prior to the first meeting, to enable the creditor to make use of the proof.

A question has been raised whether this rule is not *ultra vires;* under Sched. I. (8) it is sufficient for voting purposes to lodge it at any time prior to the time appointed for the meeting.

Rule 171 substantially corresponds with Rule 75 of the Rules of 1870.

Rule 173 requires the trustee to admit or reject wholly or in part any proof, or to require further evidence in support within fourteen days; while Rule 174 most strictly limits the appeal from such decision to twenty-one days from the date of its delivery.

This alters the former Rule, according to which no specific time was fixed for admission or rejection, and the appeal was within fourteen days after receipt of notice.

Dividends. RULES 175—177.

The following three Rules, dealing with the subject of dividends, are to be read in conjunction with sects. 58, 63 (declaration and distribution of dividends), pp. 124—127) ; sect. 162 (unclaimed and undistributed dividends or funds under this and former Acts), p. 220.

Rule 175 corresponds to some extent to Rules 131 *et seq.* of the Rules of 1870, and contains elaborate provisions as to notice, &c.

Notice of the intended dividend is to be given to the Board of Trade not more than two months nor less than twenty-one days before its declaration ; and appeals from the Master's decision must, in the absence of special extension of time by the Court, be within seven days. By Rule 176, all bills, &c. must as heretofore (Rule 134 of Rules of 1870) be exhibited to the trustee, but this regulation is now subject to (1) the provisions of sect. 70 of the Bills of Exchange Act as to lost bills, and (2) the Court's power on special grounds to dispense with production.

Discharge. RULES 178—182.

The following five Rules, dealing with the question of discharge, are to be read in conjunction with sect. 28 (discharge of bankrupt), p. 53 ; sect. 30 (effect of order of discharge), p. 60 ; sect. 99 (jurisdiction in bankruptcy of registrar), p. 163; sect. 32 (2) (disqualifications of bankrupt), p. 63; sect. 122 (power of County Court to make administration order instead of order for payment by instalments), p. 189; sect. 150 (certain provisions to bind the Crown), p. 211.

Rules 179 and 180 correspond to a considerable extent with Rules 139 and 141 of the Rules of 1870. A considerable change has been introduced into the practice as to discharge. The bankrupt must now obtain (1) from the official receiver a certificate specifying the number of his creditors; (2) a longer notice, viz., twenty-eight days, must now be given; (3) and to the official receiver as well as the trustee; (4) all the creditors must have notice fourteen days before the time appointed. Rules 181 and 182, dealing with judgments in case of conditional discharge and accounts of after-acquired property, are new, and inserted in consequence of the novel provisions of sect. 28 (6), p. 55.

Proxies and Voting Letters. RULE 183.

This Rule, dealing with proxies and voting letters, is to be read in conjunction with sect. 18 (power for creditors to accept, and Court to approve, composition or arrangement), p. 29; Schedule I. (meetings of creditors), p. 237. Note an important difference between this Rule and that in Schedule I. (Rule 19). The Rule in the schedule says before the meeting, while the present Rule prescribes the day before the meeting.

Meetings of Creditors. RULES 184—190.

The following seven Rules, dealing with the subject of the meeting of creditors, are to be read in conjunction with sect. 15 (first or other meeting of creditors), p. 23; sect. 18 (composition or scheme of arrangement), p. 29; and Schedule I. (meetings of creditors).

These Rules correspond to a certain extent with Rules 97 *et seq.* of the Rules of 1870; and the times of the various notices are now definitely fixed.

Rule 188 enables the solicitor in the matter, or his

clerk, to give proof as to sending the notice, while the re-payment of costs of calling a meeting (Rule 189) at the instance of any person other than the official receiver or trustee, is now left to the discretion of the creditors or the Court.

By Rule 190 all resolutions must now be filed.

Proceedings by Company or Co-Partnership.
Rule 191.

This Rule, dealing with proceedings to be taken by a company or co-partnership, is to be read in conjunction with sect. 148. The Rule corresponds substantially with Rule 15 of the Rules of 1870, except that the provision enabling the affidavit in support to be made by the director or other officer is here, possibly *per incuriam,* omitted.

Proceedings by or against Firm.
Rules 192—197.

The following six Rules, dealing with proceedings by or against a firm, are to be read in conjunction with the sections of the Act collected and noted under sect. 40 (1), p. 81. Rule 192, requiring the partner, when signing for the firm, to add his individual signature. Rule 193 (as to service, borrowed from Ord. IX. r. 6, Rules of the Supreme Court), and the remaining four Rules, all of which proceed on the principle of the individual responsibility of each of the partners, are new.

—◆—

Part III.—Special Procedure.

Small Bankruptcies. Rules 198, 199.

These Rules, dealing with the question of small bankruptcies, are to be read in conjunction with sect. 121 (summary administration in small cases), p. 187.

Rule 199 enumerates various provisions modifying

the characteristics of a summary administration.   The
principal points are that there is to be—

   (1) No advertisement;
   (2) No jury;
   (3) Summary power of adjudication by Court;
   (4) No appeal except by leave;
   (5) Only one meeting, except for the purpose of con-
       firming the composition or scheme; and, if
       possible, only one dividend.

See, as to adjudication, Rules 155—158, and note
thereon, *ante*, p. 310.

The first two of the three sets of circumstances enume-
rated, Rule 199 (3), under which the Court may adjudge
a debtor a bankrupt, are the same as those mentioned in
Rule 156 for ordinary adjudication; the last, *i. e.*, in cases
when the composition or scheme is not reasonable, &c.,
corresponds to that mentioned in the Act (sect. 18 (6)).

Note that the lower scale of costs prescribed by
Rule 103, *ante*, p. 303, applies to small bankruptcies.

Administration of Estate of Person dying Insolvent.   RULES 200—202.

These three Rules, dealing with the novel administration of the estates of persons dying insolvent, are to be
read in conjunction with sect. 125 (administration in
bankruptcy of estate of persons dying insolvent) p. 194,
and see note, p. 197.   See as to service, Rules 79—83.

Part IV.—Officers, Trustees, Audit, &c.

Gazetting.   RULES 203, 204.

The heading of the Queen's printer's copy, " Books to
be kept and Returns to be made by Registrars," is ob-
viously out of place, as it ought to come *after* Rule 204.

Rule 203, dealing with the question of Gazetting
notices, is to be read in conjunction with sect. 13 (ad-

vertisement of receiving order), p. 22; sect. 20 (2) (adjudication of bankruptcy where composition not accepted or approved), p. 38; sect. 132 (Gazette to be evidence), p. 202; sect. 35 (3) (power of Court to annul adjudication in certain cases), p. 67; sect. 17 (1) (public examination of debtor), p. 27; sect. 121 (summary administration in small cases), p. 187; sect. 125 (administration in bankruptcy of estate of person dying insolvent), p. 194; sect. 18 (3) (power for creditors to accept and Court to approve composition or arrangement), p. 30.

Books to be kept and Returns to be made by Registrars.   RULES 205, 206.

These Rules substantially correspond with Rules 240 and 241 of the Rules of 1870, with the exception that the extracts, returns and other information are now to be furnished to the Board of Trade.

Accounts and Audit.   RULES 207—217.

These eleven Rules, dealing with the question of accounts and audit, are to be read in conjunction with sect. 80 (books to be kept by trustee), p. 146; sect. 78 (audit of trustees' accounts), p. 145; sect. 82 (release of trustee), p. 147; sect. 40 (3) (priority of debts), p. 79; sect. 81 (annual statement of proceedings), p. 147.

See note to sect. 78, p. 145, where the distinctions between the law as to audit of trustees' accounts under the Bankruptcy Act, 1869, and the present Act are pointed out.

Rules 207, 208, 211, 213 and 214, as to the keeping of the record book (formerly "record") and cash book (formerly "estate book") and the audit of the accounts, &c., substantially correspond with Rules 242 *et seq.* of the Rules of 1870, Rule 15 of the Rules of 1871, with the additions as to the official receiver and Board of Trade.

The provisions as to the audit by the Board of Trade

(211), the filing of accounts (212), the distinct accounts of joint and separate estates (215), the disposal of debtors' books (216), and the annual returns to the Board of Trade (217) are new.

Trustees.   RULES 218—231.

The fourteen Rules dealing with the position of trustees are to be read in conjunction with sect. 21 (appointment of trustee), and sects. 72—91, Part V. of the Act (trustees in bankruptcy).

Rules 218 *et seq.* provide as to form of gazetting, &c., of the certificate of appointment, and as to the notification of objection by the Board of Trade to the High Court under sect. 21 (3), and see note, p. 41. The report of the Board of Trade is of itself, like the official receiver's report under sect. 28 (4), to be *primâ facie* evidence of the truth of the statements contained in it. Non-compliance with sect. 162, or any order under it, is to be of itself a fatal objection to a trustee's appointment. The next two Rules (222 and 223) prescribe the practice as to the removal and resignation of trustees. Rule 224 deals with the question of remuneration on the new principle (see pp. 136 and 137), and provides that separate accounts are to be kept of amounts realized and distributed, and that the percentage on the former is not to exceed that on the latter. By Rule 225, a trustee carrying on business (see notes to sects. 57 and 64) is to keep distinct accounts, and verify them by affidavit at least once a month. Notice of the application to the Board of Trade for a release must be given to the creditors who have proved, and must be accompanied by a summary of receipts and payments. By Rule 227 meetings to consider the question of removing a trustee may be summoned if one-fourth in value of the creditors desire it and a deposit to cover expenses be made. Rules 228 and 229 supply the forms for application for accounts in local banks and directions. Rules 230 and 231 fix the fees for copies of accounts and list of creditors at three pence per folio.

Disclaimer of Lease. RULE 232.

This Rule, dealing with the question of disclaimer of a lease, is to be read in conjunction with sect. 55 (disclaimer of onerous property), p. 112; and see Introductory Chapter, p. lxviii.

A lease may be disclaimed without leave in any one of three cases, *i. e.* (1) when under 20*l.* value; or (2) in summary administrations; or (3) when lessor, after notice, does not require the matter to be brought before the Court. In all these cases, however, it is essential that the bankrupt should not have either sub-let or assigned or mortgaged or charged the lease in question.

Official Receivers. RULES 233—250.

These eighteen Rules, dealing with the question of official receivers, are to be read in conjunction with sects. 66—71, Part IV. of the Act (official receivers and staff of Board of Trade), pp. 129—135.

By Rule 233 judicial notice is to be taken of the appointment of official receivers (and of those of their official assistants, Rule 242), while the subsequent Rules deal with the appointment of deputies and the removal, &c. and rotation of official receivers.

A variety of new powers and duties are here conferred and imposed on official receivers, in addition to those mentioned in sects. 68—70, pp. 131—135 :—

1. To furnish instructions to the debtor for the preparation of his statement of affairs. (Rule 237 (1).)
2. To hold forthwith a personal interview with the debtor, for the purpose of investigating his affairs and deciding whether the case is a proper one for a summary administration under sect. 121; and note that the official receiver may depute some person (*i. e.* apparently *any* person) to discharge this duty for him. (Rule 237 (2).)
3. To make an allowance to the bankrupt while in possession of his property (Rule 233) similar to that which may be at a subsequent stage made

    to the bankrupt with the consent of the committee of inspection, under sect. 64, sub-sect. 2. (See note thereon.)

4. To make a special report, &c. to the Board of Trade whenever he employs any one to assist the debtor in the preparation of his statement of affairs. (Rule 239.)

5. To depute by writing some person (a) in his employment; or (b) under his official control; or (c) some officer of the Board of Trade, to use proxies entrusted to him. (Rule 240.)

6. To remove a special manager if his employment be (a) unnecessary; or (b) unprofitable; or (c) if so required by a special resolution of the creditors. (Rule 244.)

7. To apply to the Court for directions in any case of (a) doubt or difficulty; or (b) when any matter is not provided for by the Act or Rules. (Rule 246.)

    Applications to the Court may be made personally, informally and without notice, subject to the power of the Court to order their renewal formally and with notice. (Rule 245.)

8. On adjudication to transfer (a) property, and (b) communicate all necessary information to the trustee. (Rule 247.)

9. To account to the debtor or trustee, in the cases mentioned in Rule 249. If the account be unsatisfactory a report may be made to the Board of Trade, but it is expressly provided by Rule 249 (4) that the provisions as to trustees' accounts are not to apply to official receivers when acting as trustees (see note, p. 130), but that they are to account as the Board of Trade may direct.

10. To perform the functions of the Board of Trade, subject to their discretion in cases where there is no committee of inspection. (Rule 250.)

Other points covered by this group of Rules are that the Board of Trade may determine what acts or duties must be done personally by the official receiver, and what they may delegate to persons in their regular employ or under their official control. (Rule 241.) The registrar is to act as official receiver in cases of emergency. (Rule 243.) In cases where there are available assets the official receivers need not incur any expense without the express direction of the Board of Trade. (Rule 248.)

Payments into and out of Bank.

RULES 251, 252.

These two Rules, dealing with the questions of payments into and out of a local bank (p. 51) and payments out of the Bank of England, are to be read in conjunction with sect. 74 (payment of money into Bank of England), p. 140; and see sub-sect. 4, as to local bank, and note, p. 142, and sect. 75 (trustee not to pay into private account), p. 143.

Note that all cheques must be payable to order. The local bank cheque must be (1) marked on its face with the name of the estate, (2) signed by the trustee, and (3) countersigned by some person appointed by the creditors or committee of inspection. Payments out of the Bankruptcy Estates Account (Bank of England), sect. 74, must be signed by the appointed officers of the Board of Trade.

Security by Trustee or Special Manager.

RULE 253.

This Rule, dealing with the question of security to be given by trustee or special manager, is to be read in conjunction with sect. 21 (2) (appointment of trustee), p. 39; sect. 12 (2) (power to appoint special manager), p. 21. Note that the Rule only prescribes that the security may be given either specially or generally, and anything else is left completely to the discretion of the Board of Trade.

Remuneration of Special Manager. RULE 254.

This Rule, dealing with the question of the remuneration of special manager when it is not fixed by the
creditors, is to be read in conjunction with sect. 12 (3)
(power to appoint special manager), p. 22. The remuneration, unless fixed by the creditors, is to be according to such scale as the Board may fix from time to
time.

Unclaimed Funds, &c., under Sect. 162.
RULES 255, 256.

These two Rules, dealing with unclaimed funds, &c., are
to be read in conjunction with sect. 162 (unclaimed and
undistributed dividends or funds under this and former
acts), p. 220. Note that both Rules seem to contemplate the future issue by the Board of directions as to
paying-in orders and applications for paying out.

Part V.—Miscellaneous.

Miscellaneous Matters. RULES 257—264.

These eight Rules, dealing with a variety of miscellaneous matters, cannot be said specially to refer to any
particular portions of the act. Rule 257 gives the
Board of Trade a general power to issue rules of an
administrative, and not judicial character, just as Rule 4
enabled it to issue forms of a similar nature. Judicial
notice is to be taken of all general orders or regulations
which are printed by the Queen's printer and purport to
be issued under the authority of the Board of Trade.

Falsification of documents is, in addition to any
other penalty, to be treated as a contempt of Court.
(Rule 258.) No lien (as under Rule 110 of the Rules
of 1870) is to be allowed on the debtor's books. (Rule
259.) The next Rule, providing that non-compliance
with Rules is not to render proceedings void, is bor-

rowed from the Rules of the Supreme Court, Ord. LXX.
r. 1. (Rule 260.) The Court has a power similar to that in
Rules of the Supreme Court, Ord. LXIV. r. 7, to abridge
or enlarge time ; but note that here it is only to be done
under special circumstances, and for good cause shown,
and that there is no provision that the application may
be made, though the time allowed or appointed has ex-
pired. (Rule 261.) The old Bankruptcy Rules under the
Act of 1869 are repealed, except as to pending proceedings.
(Rule 262.) Rule 263 contains two extremely important
provisions: (1) saving the existing (*i.e.*, the old) law, procedure and practice in bankruptcy matters when no provision
is made by the present Act or Rules; and (2) providing
that the Rules of the Supreme Court are not to apply
to proceedings in bankruptcy, unless as provided by
the present or some amending Rules. Registrars are
in pending proceedings under old Acts to retain all
the powers and jurisdiction which they had by delega-
tion or otherwise, unless there be express provision or
order to the contrary.   (Rule 264.)

RULES under Sect. 5 of the Debtors Act, 1869, and Sect. 103 of the Act.

RULES 265—270.

The following six Rules deal with the question of
judgment debtors, and are to be read with sect. 103,
p. 169.. And see p. 171 *et sequitur.*

The bankruptcy registrars of the High Court are to
exercise jurisdiction unless and until the Lord Chancellor
otherwise orders.   (Rule 265.)

The same fee and deposit are to be paid in respect of
a receiving order under the new power conferred by
sect. 103; and, in the event of non-payment, the Court
may dismiss or adjourn the application.   (Rule 266.)

An important power is conferred on the County
Courts in cases where the total liabilities do not exceed

50*l.*, to make an administration order under sect. 122; as to which, see the special code, *post*, p. 324. (Rule 267.)

The remaining Rules (268, 269, 270) provide for transfer where the application to commit is made to a judge who has not bankruptcy jurisdiction; that inferior Courts within the London bankruptcy district shall not have jurisdiction in respect of High Court judgments, and that the County Court Rules as to procedure for committal, shall, with any necessary modifications, apply to all Courts exercising the jurisdiction in question.

RULES

ADMINISTRATION ORDERS under SECT. 122.

A SEPARATE body of Rules and Forms deals with the administration orders, which the County Courts are now empowered to make under sects. 122 (pp. 189 and 192 *et sequitur*), in cases where the total indebtedness does not exceed 50*l*.

Rule 1 prescribes how the request is to be filed. Rule 2 enables a debtor forthwith, after a judgment has been obtained against him, to have the proceedings stayed in order to enable him to file the request. Notice of the time when the application is to be heard is to be given to the debtor, and to all scheduled creditors. Rule 4 deals with objections to any of the scheduled debts.

The course of proceedings on the hearing is prescribed by Rule 5. The principal points are—(a) As to the personal attendance of the debtor; (b) right of any creditor to attend and prove; (c) schedule to be sufficient proof of debts, unless objected to; (d) power of adjournment in case of disputed claims; (g) the novel and stringent power conferred upon the Court of taking into consideration the circumstances under which the indebtedness was incurred, and particularly whether the same or any part thereof was incurred by means of fraud, and whether the debtor has been guilty of idleness, improvidence, gambling or intemperance. A copy of the order is to be sent to the debtor, and notice to each creditor. (Rule 6.)

Objections by creditors are dealt with by Rules 7 and 8. Rules 9, 10, 11, deal with the claims of creditors who were omitted from the schedule, or became creditors subsequent to the order.

Rule 12 enables the Court (a) if it thinks fit, or (b) if the majority of creditors desire it, to appoint any person (*i. e.* not necessarily a creditor) to have the conduct of the order; such person may be removed by the Court at any time, and in case of his neglect to take proceedings, or of urgency, any creditor may take proceedings.

Rule 13 deals with the enforcement of the order by judgment summons, which shall be issued without fee; the burthen of proof is now shifted (see sect. 122 (6), pp. 190, 193), and the debtor must prove his inability to pay. The Court, however, has a power of suspending the administration order if the debtor has not the means to pay.

Rule 14 prescribes the circumstances under which the Court may suspend or vary its orders.

By Rule 15 the administration order is to be suspended if the execution of the order for committal is suspended; and (Rule 16) instalments accruing due are not to be reckoned during the suspension of the administration order.

Rule 17 deals with the positions of persons who became creditors subsequent to the order; and by Rule 18 the registrar is to keep such accounts of receipts and payments as the Commissioners of the Treasury may direct.

TABLE OF FEES OF DECEMBER 28, 1883.

The Lord Chancellor, with the concurrence of the Treasury, has appointed the following Table of Fees to be paid on proceedings under "The Bankruptcy Act, 1883."

Scale of Solicitor's Costs.

Petitioning Creditor's Bill of Costs to the Issue of Receiving Order.

	£	s.	d.
Instructions for petition	1	0	0
Examining witnesses as to act of bankruptcy	0	10	0
Examining particulars of petitioning creditor's account	0	6	8

The act of bankruptcy being a declaration admitting inability to pay, filed by the solicitor to the petitioner, or an assignment prepared by the solicitor to the petitioner, or default made upon a bankruptcy notice issued by the solicitor to the petitioner, these two last charges will not be allowed. The expense of an assignment will not be allowed where a declaration of inability would answer the purpose.

If solicitor reside at a distance :—

Writing agent to search for prior petition	3s. 6d.
Agent's writing result of search	3s. 6d.

	£	s.	d.
Searching if prior petition filed	0	7	8
Drawing bankruptcy petition, including order for hearing	0	10	0

Ingrossing same, 4d. per folio only to be allowed where the petition exceeds seven folios.

	£	s.	d.
Paid for stamp	5	0	0
Attesting signature of each petitioner, except in case of partnership	0	6	8
Drawing and fair copy affidavit verifying petition	0	3	4
Attending petitioner to be sworn	0	6	8
Paid oath (if paid)			

Two copies of petition for sealing, 4d. per folio.

	£	s.	d.
Preparing subpœna and serving witnesses, or arranging with witnesses for their attendance on presentation of petition	0	13	4
Paid them			

See Witnesses' Scale. Petitioning creditor is not to be regarded as a witness, and is not to be paid for loss of time; he may claim his expenses of travelling and subsistence.

	£	s.	d.
Attending on presentation of petition when court investigated statements therein, and clerk	1	0	0

One fee only for attending will be allowed, unless by direction of the court at the time, and a memorandum of its allowance produced to the taxing officer.

	£	s.	d.
Drawing order for hearing of petition	0	3	4

Service of petition (see General Rules).

	£	s.	d.
Attending court on hearing (where debtor does not appear or dispute)	0	10	0

Debtors' Bill of Costs where Debtor petitions.

	£	s.	d.
Instructions for petition	1	0	0
Drawing and attesting petition	0	13	4
Paid stamp	5	0	0
Attending filing	0	6	8

Where Act of Bankruptcy the filing a Declaration of inability to Pay.

	£	s.	d.
Drawing and attesting declaration of inability to pay	0	13	4
Paid stamp	0	5	1
Attending filing	0	6	8

Cost of Bankruptcy Notice.

	£	s.	d.
Instructions for, and preparing notice	0	6	8
Preparing request for issue	0	6	8
Attending filing	0	6	8
Paid for office copy			
Notice and two fair copies	0	6	8
Attending sealing notice, copies	0	6	8
Paid stamp	0	5	0
Service of notice	0	5	0
Attending court on hearing of notice	0	13	4

Costs where the Debtor is required by the Court to enter into a Bond.

	£	s.	d.
Attending making inquiries as to sufficiency of sureties	0	13	4

This charge will be subject to increase, according to the distance of the sureties' residence ; and, where necessary, agency charges for making such inquiries.

	£	s.	d.
Drawing exceptions to sureties	0	3	4
Service thereof on debtor's solicitor	0	5	0
Attending court when sureties allowed or disallowed	0	13	4

Costs of affidavits in opposition to the allowance of the bond for want of sufficiency of sureties, the same allowance as for other special affidavits.

Costs of Bankruptcy Notice, where the Court allows Costs to Debtor on Notice set Aside.

The debtor's personal expenses for travelling and loss of time, according to the scale allowed to witnesses.

And if attended by a solicitor, and his costs allowed (which must be by special order of the court).

	£	s.	d.
Instructions to attend the court on the notice	0	6	8
Affidavit of counterclaim, &c.............	0	2	6
Paid stamp	0	1	0
Attending court on hearing of notice, and drawing up order	0	13	4
Attending for appointment to tax, and copy and service of order and appointment	0	5	0
Attending taxing	0	6	8
Paid allocatur stamp			

Costs of Application to prosecute a Petition in a particular District, or to transfer Petition from one District to another.

	£	s.	d.
Instructions for affidavit to ground application	0	6	8
Drawing same, 1s. per folio.			
Fair copy, 4d. per folio.			
Attending deponent to be sworn.......................	0	6	8
Paid oath			
Attending court when order made, and drawing up same..	0	13	4

Costs on Application for Warrant.

	£	s.	d.
Instructions for affidavit in support of application for warrant...	0	6	8
Drawing same, per folio 1s.			
Fair copy, per folio 4d.			
Attending to read over and to get same sworn.............	0	6	8
Attending court, warrant granted	0	13	4
Fair copy, per folio 4d.			
Attending officer, instructing him as to the execution of the warrant..	0	6	8

Costs of disputing Statements in Petition.

	£	s.	d.
Attending debtor served with copy of petition, taking instructions to show cause against same	0	6	8
Drawing notice showing cause	0	5	0
Two fair copies for service	0	2	0
Service on creditor including postage	0	3	6
Ditto registrar	0	3	6
Perusing and considering petition	0	6	8
Examining witnesses in opposition	0	10	0
Costs of brief, and counsel's fee, where requisite to employ counsel.			
Attending court	1	0	0

Petitioning Creditor's Costs on Bankrupt disputing Statements in Petition.

	£	s.	d.
The debtor having served notice of disputing the statements in petition, attending petitioner	0	6	8
Special attendances will be allowed to examine witnesses as to the facts they can prove, the charges for which, and for summoning them, will be in the discretion of the taxing officer, according to the circumstances; and where necessary to employ counsel to support the petition, the usual charges for brief and counsel's fees will be allowed.			
Attending court when receiving order made..............	1	0	0

B.B.   A A

*Costs for substituted Service where Debtor keeps out of the
way to avoid Service.*

Several attendances to serve without effect, when it appearing that the debtor was keeping out of the way, and could not be personally served, instructions to apply for substituted service	0	6	8

£   *s.*   *d.*

Several attendances to serve without effect, when it appearing that the debtor was keeping out of the way, and could not be personally served, instructions to apply for substituted service 0 6 8

Drawing affidavit of facts, and that due pains had been taken to effect personal service, per folio 1*s.*

Fair copy, 4*d.* per folio.

Attending court for order for substituted service, and drawing up order 0 13 4

Costs of Brief.

Instructions for brief in discretion of taxing officer (allowed only when counsel employed) ....

Drawing same, 1*s.* per folio.

Fair copy, 4*d.* per folio.

Fee to counsel and clerk...................................

Attending him... 0 6 8

Where consultation or conference is necessary, attending to appoint same 0 6 8

Fee to counsel and clerk ....

Attending consultation or conference.................... 0 13 4

Cost of Cases for opinion of Counsel.

Instructions for case 0 6 8

Drawing same, 1*s.* per folio.

Fair copy, 4*d.* per folio.

Fee to counsel and clerk ....

Attending him... 0 6 8

Where conference is necessary attending to appoint same.. 0 6 8

Fee to counsel and clerk attending conference 0 13 4

Attending for and perusing opinion 0 6 8

Attending client, reading over opinion, and conferring with him thereon 0 6 8

Costs of Motion.

Instructions 0 6 8

Where on appeal... 0 13 4

Drawing notice of motion to be served, per folio, 1*s.*

Fair copies, 4*d.* per folio.

Perusing documents (by London agent) on an appeal from £1 : 1*s.* to £2 : 2*s.*

Making copy for filing of notice of motion, and attending registrar therewith, previously to the sitting of the court 0 3 4

Instructions for affidavit in support of motion............ 0 3 4

[No instructions allowed where the solicitor or his clerk makes the affidavit; no fees allowed to counsel to settle affidavit, unless very special.]

Drawing same, at per folio 1*s.*

Fair copies, per folio 4*d.*

Attending reading over and to be sworn 0 6 8

	£	s.	d.
Paid oath			
Copy affidavit for service with the notice of motion, 4*d*. per folio.			
Service, see General Rules.			
Attending to file affidavit.................................	0	6	8
Paid for office copy, when required			
Affidavit of service and copy notice of motion to annex'....	0	6	8
Attending court on motion if heard £1 : 1*s*., and if not	0	10	6
Drawing order, per folio 1*s*.			
Attending settling same	0	13	4
Fair copy, per folio 4*d*.			
Attending to pass order...................................	0	6	8
Copy to serve, where necessary, per folio 4*d*.			

GENERAL RULES.

1. More than one attendance at presentation or hearing of bankruptcy petition will not be allowed unless ordered by the court, and memorandum be obtained to that effect.

2. Attendance upon the court for necessary purposes not included in the foregoing scale, each **0 6 8**

   Attending court on each sitting (including presentation and hearing of petition)........................... **1 0 0**

       If by agent **2 0 0**

   Clerk's attendance at each sitting, when required **0 5 0**

3. Service of petition, order, notice, or other process, each service **0 5 0**

       If the distance be more than three miles, 5*d*. per mile extra, or a further sum, in the discretion of the taxing officer, according to circumstances.

       In cases of great distance, the service must be by agent, unless otherwise sanctioned.

4. Drawing and copy bill of costs, per folio **0 0 4**

5. General attendances, each **0 6 8**

   Long and special attendances **0 13 4**

       (Or more, in the discretion of the taxing officer.)

6. Writing letters, each, special **0 5 0**

       Ditto, common.................................. **0 3 6**

7. Circular letters, if above twenty ....each **0 1 0**

   If numerous, they must be printed.

8. Attendances to insert advertisements **0 3 4**

9. Extra allowances for length of sittings, or other increased allowances must have the sanction of the court, and a memorandum to that effect obtained, or all such charges will be disallowed.

10. Vouchers must be produced on taxation for all payments, or they will be disallowed.

11. Bills of costs must be written lengthwise, on one side only, *and dates must be furnished to each item*, such dates not to be written in the margin, which is to be left clear for taxation.

12. In special cases, where counsel are not instructed to appear in court, a charge by the solicitor for the preparation of minutes of fact or evidence for his own use may be allowed.

N.B.—Other necessary matters not herein provided for may be allowed on a similar scale, as nearly as may be, or in accordance with the practice of the Supreme Court, according to the nature of the proceeding.

The allowances to witnesses shall be the same as in the High Court.

The following charges to the end shall be subject to reduction by agreement with the trustee, or increase with the sanction of the committee of inspection and official receiver :—

	£	s.	d.	
Broker's Allowances.				
For inventory only—for every £100 or part of £100	0	10	0	
For inventory and valuation of chattel property—				
For the first £100	2	10	0	per cent.
For the next £400	1	10	0	,,
All above up to £10,000	1	0	0	,,
Above £10,000	0	10	0	,,
For sales by private contract based on valuation..	0	10	0	,,
For sales by auction of chattel property, including all expenses except advertisements, which must in each case be authorized by the official receiver or the trustee, not exceeding—				
For the first £100	10	0	0	,,
For the next £400	7	10	0	,,
For the next £500	6	0	0	,,
All above £1,000	5	0	0	,,

No higher allowance to be sanctioned without leave of the Board of Trade.

Costs of Surveys, Dilapidations, and Specifications.
From £2 to £5 in discretion of taxing officer.

	£	s.	d.
Accountant's Charges.			
For preparing balance-sheet, investigating accounts, &c., principal's time exclusively so employed, per day of seven hours, including necessary affidavit, or such other sum as the court may under special circumstances order	1 to 5	1 to 5	0 to 0
Chief clerk's time	0 to 1	10 to 11	6 to 6
Other clerk's time, per day of seven hours	0 to 0	7 to 16	6 to 0

These charges to include stationery, except the forms used.

Selborne, C.

J. *Chamberlain,*

President of the Board of Trade.

SEALS OF COURTS.

THE BANKRUPTCY ACT, 1883.

I, THE RIGHT HONOURABLE ROUNDELL, EARL OF SELBORNE, Lord High Chancellor of Great Britain, Do hereby, by virtue of the power vested in me by the Bankruptcy Act, 1883, Order that the High Court shall, from and after the 1st day of January, 1884, have and use in respect of bankruptcy proceedings therein a seal describing such court as "The Supreme Court of Judicature, Bankruptcy;" and that every county court shall, from and after the time aforesaid, have and use the same seal as heretofore.

Selborne, C.

FEES AND PER-CENTAGES.

THE BANKRUPTCY ACT, 1883.

I, THE RIGHT HONOURABLE ROUNDELL, EARL OF SELBORNE, Lord High Chancellor of Great Britain, Do, by virtue of the powers vested in me by the Bankruptcy Act, 1883, prescribe that the fees and per-centages in the scales hereto annexed shall, from and after the first day of January, 1884, be the fees and per-centages to be charged for or in respect of proceedings under the said Act, and shall be taken in any court having jurisdiction in bankruptcy and in any office connected with any such court, and in the Board of Trade and any office connected therewith, and by any officer paid wholly or partly out of public moneys attached to any such court or to the Board of Trade.

Selborne, C.

SCALE OF FEES AND PER-CENTAGES.

TABLE A.

	Amount.		
	£	s.	d.
Every declaration by a debtor of inability to pay his debts .	0	5	0
Every bankruptcy notice	0	5	0
Every bankruptcy petition	5	0	0
Every bond with sureties	0	10	0
Every affidavit filed, other than proof of debts	0	2	0
Every subpœna not exceeding three persons	0	5	0
For taking an affidavit or an affirmation, or attestation, upon honour in lieu of an affidavit or declaration, except for proof of debts, for each person making the same	0	1	6
And in addition thereto for each exhibit therein referred to and required to be marked	0	1	0
On every proof of debt	0	1	0
For every witness sworn and examined by an officer of the court or Board of Trade in his office, unless otherwise provided, including oath, for each hour or part of an hour ..	0	10	0
For an examination of witnesses by any such officer away from the office (in addition to reasonable travelling and other expenses) per day	3	0	0
Every petition under section 125 of the Act	5	0	0
Every special proxy or voting paper	0	0	6
Every receiving order under section 103 of the Act	5	0	0

	£	s.	d.

Every application for an order of discharge .... — 2 0 0
   And for each creditor to be notified.................. — 0 1 0

Every application to the court under sections 18 and 23 to approve a scheme, a fee computed at the rate of £1 upon the first £100 or fraction of £100 and 5s. upon each £25 or fraction thereof above £100 on the gross amount of the estimated assets. — —

Every application to the court under sections 18 and 23 to approve a composition, a fee computed at the rate of £1 upon the first £100 or fraction of £100, and 5s. upon each £25 or fraction thereof above £100 on the gross amount of the composition. — —

Every application for search other than by a petitioner, trustee, banker, or officer of the court.................... — 0 1 0

Every application to a court, except by the official receiver. — 0 5 0

Every office copy, each folio of 72 words .... — 0 0 4

On every record of trial .... — 5 0 0
   or such less sum as the court may specially order.

Every allocatur by any officer of the court for any costs, charges or disbursements, where the amount allowed shall not exceed £4 .... — 0 2 0

Where the amount exceeds £4, for every £2 allowed, or a fraction thereof .... — 0 1 0

Table B.

Every application to an official receiver to appoint a special manager .... — 0 5 0

Every application by a committee of inspection to the Board of Trade for a local banking account .... — 1 0 0

Every order of the Board of Trade for a local banking account .... — 2 0 0

On one copy of the cash book, showing assets realised, forwarded for audit by the official receiver or trustee, to the Board of Trade, a fee at the rate of £1 upon the first £100 or fraction thereof, and 5s. upon each £25 or fraction thereof beyond £100 on the gross amount of the assets realised and brought to credit. This fee is not to be charged where a fee has been taken on an application under sections 18 or 23.

Every application under section 162 to the Board of Trade for payment of money out of the bankruptcy estates account 2s. 6d.

Table C.

	£	s.	d.

High bailiff attending court each sitting .... — 0 2 0

Serving every bankruptcy notice, bankruptcy petition, or subpoena within two miles, including affidavit of service — 0 3 6

Executing every warrant of seizure, or search warrant, or warrant of apprehension, or order of commitment within two miles of court house.................................. — 0 10 0

<table>
<tr><td></td><td>£</td><td>s.</td><td>d.</td></tr>
</table>

Keeping possession under a warrant—for each day the man is actually in possession ; including affidavit of possession being actually kept 0 4 6

    (not less than 3*s.* 6*d.* of the above sum is to be paid to the man in possession, and his receipt produced.)

High bailiff's, or (in the London Bankruptcy District) officer's, man travelling to place of possession, or to execute a warrant of or order of commitment, or to serve a summons or subpœna, or for any other purpose specially directed by the court, per mile......................... 0 0 5

His time, per day, where distance exceeds ten miles 0 4 6

His expenses, per day   ,,   ,,   ,, ... 0 4 6

If high bailiff of a county court or bankruptcy officer of Supreme Court directed by the court personally to travel, per mile 0 0 7

If high bailiff of a county court or bankruptcy officer of Supreme Court directed by the court personally to travel, his time, per day...................................... 0 10 0

If high bailiff of a county court or bankruptcy officer of Supreme Court directed by the court personally to travel, his expenses, per day................................... 0 10 0

Table D.

On the net assets realised or brought to credit by the official receiver, whether acting as interim receiver or as trustee, not being assets received and spent in carrying on the business of the debtor, £6 per cent.

On every payment under section 162 of money out of the bankruptcy estates account, 5*s.* on each £20 *ad valorem* on the amount paid.

<table>
<tr><td></td><td>£</td><td>s.</td><td>d.</td></tr>
</table>

Room for meeting of creditors, summoned by official receiver, for each creditor present personally or by proxy at each meeting 0 1 0

For each notice to creditor of a meeting.................. 0 1 0

Keeping possession, per day.............................. 0 4 6

Travelling, and other reasonable expenses of official receiver

For official stationery, books, and forms, each estate, for every fifty creditors, or less 1 0 0

Table E.

For every order of administration under section 122, two shillings in the pound on the total amount of the debts scheduled from time to time, excluding any fraction of a pound in such total.

TABLE F.

The fees and allowances payable on proceedings had after the thirty-first day of December, 1883, in respect of any matter which was pending in any court having jurisdiction in bankruptcy on the said day shall be the same as if those proceedings had been taken before such day, and shall be applied to the same purposes.

WE, the undersigned Lords Commissioners of her Majesty's Treasury, do hereby sanction the foregoing scale of fees and percentages, and do direct that the fees to be taken by stamps shall be those mentioned in Tables A. and B., and that the fees mentioned in Tables C., D. and E. shall be taken in money, and that the fees and allowances referred to in Table F. shall be taken by stamps or money, according as they have hitherto been taken. In respect of all proceedings in the High Court of Justice and the Court of Appeal the stamps to be used shall be Judicature fee stamps; and in respect of all other proceedings the stamps to be used shall be Bankruptcy fee stamps.

And we further direct that the stamp shall be affixed or the money paid in respect of every fee before the proceeding is had in respect of which the fee is payable, and that the charge to be made by the London Gazette for the insertion of each notice authorized by the Act or Rules shall be ten shillings, except in the cases of estates administered under Part VII. of the Act, in which cases the charge shall be three shillings and fourpence.

R. W. DUFF.
H. J. GLADSTONE.

INDEX TO SUPPLEMENT.

THE

BANKRUPTCY ACT, 1883

WITH

𝕹𝖔𝖙𝖊𝖘 𝖆𝖓𝖉 𝖆𝖓 𝕴𝖓𝖙𝖗𝖔𝖉𝖚𝖈𝖙𝖔𝖗𝖞 𝕮𝖍𝖆𝖕𝖙𝖊𝖗,

AND

AN APPENDIX

CONTAINING

𝕿𝖍𝖊 𝕺𝖋𝖋𝖎𝖈𝖎𝖆𝖑 𝕺𝖗𝖉𝖊𝖗, 𝕮𝖎𝖗𝖈𝖚𝖑𝖆𝖗𝖘 𝖆𝖓𝖉 𝕱𝖔𝖗𝖒𝖘.

*(With a SUPPLEMENT containing a Table showing the parts
of the Act and Rules which are to be read together: a
Summary of the points of importance contained in
the Rules, and the* TABLE OF FEES *of
the 28th December,* 1883.)

BY

THOMAS BRETT, LL.B. London University, B.A.,

OF THE MIDDLE TEMPLE, BARRISTER-AT-LAW,

*Late Scholar and Student of Trinity College, Dublin; Exhibitioner in Real Property
and Equity; Holder of the First Certificate of Honour, Michaelmas,* 1869;
and Joint Editor of " Clerke & Brett's Conveyancing Acts."

LONDON:

BUTTERWORTHS, 7, FLEET STREET,

𝕷𝖆𝖜 𝕻𝖚𝖇𝖑𝖎𝖘𝖍𝖊𝖗𝖘 𝖙𝖔 𝖙𝖍𝖊 𝕼𝖚𝖊𝖊𝖓'𝖘 𝖒𝖔𝖘𝖙 𝖊𝖝𝖈𝖊𝖑𝖑𝖊𝖓𝖙 𝕸𝖆𝖏𝖊𝖘𝖙𝖞.

DUBLIN: HODGES, FIGGIS & CO., GRAFTON STREET.
CALCUTTA: THACKER, SPINK & CO. MELBOURNE: GEORGE ROBERTSON.
MANCHESTER: MEREDITH, RAY & LITTLER.
EDINBURGH: T. & T. CLARK; BELL & BRADFUTE.

1884

LONDON:
PRINTED BY C. F. ROWORTH, BREAM'S BUILDINGS,
CHANCERY LANE.

TO

THE RIGHT HONORABLE

ROUNDELL EARL SELBORNE,

Lord High Chancellor of Great Britain,

This Work

IS

(BY HIS LORDSHIP'S KIND PERMISSION)

MOST RESPECTFULLY DEDICATED

BY

The AUTHOR.

PREFATORY NOTE TO SUPPLEMENT.

The pages which are now presented to the public are intended as a Supplement to the Author's work on the new Bankruptcy Act itself. The official copies of the Rules and Forms can be obtained separately, at a rate so cheap, and in a form so perfect, that it has not been deemed advisable to re-print them on the present occasion. The reader will find in these supplementary pages a Tabular Statement of the various portions of the Act and Rules which are to be read together, and a summary of the points of importance contained in the Rules, which it is believed will be found sufficient to enable him to master the new Bankruptcy practice with little difficulty. The Table of Fees issued on the 28th December, 1883, under sect. 128, will be found at p. 327.

T. B.

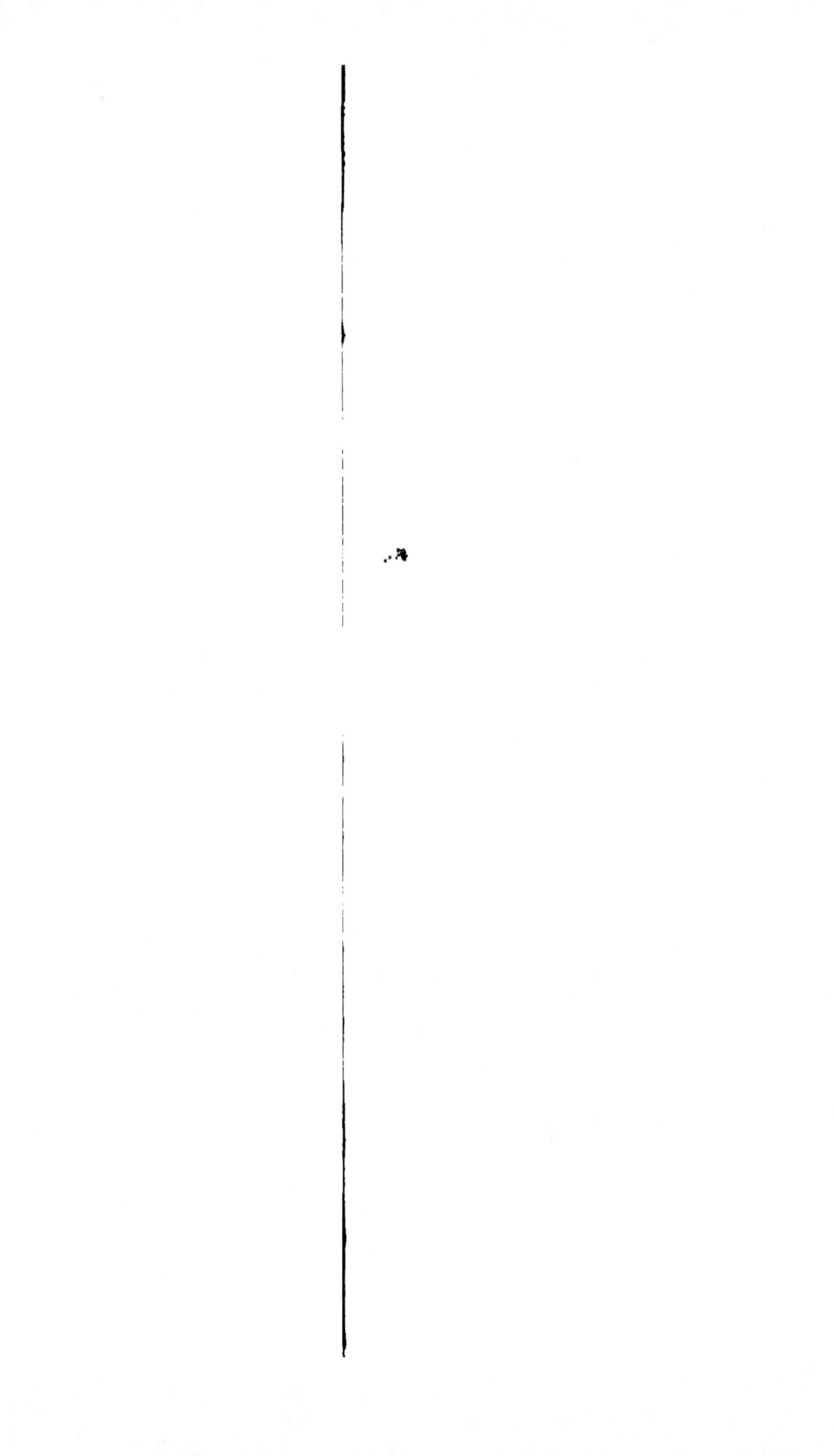